QUICK WAYS TO KEEPY THE KIDDOS BUSY

Quick Ways to Keepy The Kiddos Busy

Marianne Frandsen

Bonkers Kids

CONTENTS

TO INTRODUCE

Welcome to "Quick Ways to Keep the Kiddos Busy," a handy little pocketbook filled with fun and easy activities to keep your children entertained. I'm Marianne Frandsen, a mother of four energetic kids who have taught me the art of balancing creativity and chaos. Over the years, I've discovered countless ways to engage their curious minds and restless bodies, and I'm excited to share these ideas with you.

Whether you're looking for a quick distraction during a busy day or a creative project to spark your child's imagination, this book has something for every occasion. From indoor games to outdoor adventures, you'll find a variety of activities that are easy to set up and sure to keep your kiddos happily occupied.

Parenting is an adventure, and with the right tools, you can turn even the most hectic days into memorable experiences. Let's dive in and explore some quick and simple ways to keep your kiddos busy and, most importantly, having fun!

1

INDOOR ACTIVITIES

1. Story Time: Gather the kids for a cozy story session. Read and discuss a book or a chapter, then let their imaginations run wild by creating alternate endings. For extra fun, sit in a circle and take turns adding sentences to a made-up story. We've created some hilariously unique tales this way!

2. Giant Easel: Visit a charity shop or wallpaper store to find leftover rolls of wallpaper. Cover a wall with the paper (backside out) using blu-tack or drawing pins. Provide the kids with paints,

crayons, chalks, and pens, and let them create a giant mural. Little ones can reach the bottom, while older kids can work on the top.

3. **Wax Creations:** Give the kids old wax crayon stubs and let them shave the crayons onto a piece of wax paper using a butter knife. Once they're done, place another piece of wax paper on top and briefly press with a warm iron. Watch as the colors melt together to create beautiful patterns. Let the creations cool and harden before displaying them.

4. **Old Clothes:** Sort through your old clothes for items that don't fit or are out of fashion. Gather two cardboard boxes: one for "dress up" clothes and one for "rags." Fill the "dress up" box with the most outrageous outfits and use the other clothes for rags. Let the kids play dress-up or get creative with the rags. Endless fun awaits!

5. **Puppet Show:** Help the kids make

finger puppets from paper and create a "show" with a script and characters. Build a puppet theater from a few boxes taped together, with an opening at the front and a curtain made from rags. Let the kids practice their show until they're confident, then invite friends or family to watch the performance.

6.   **Kitchen Fun:** Browse cookbooks and let the kids choose a simple recipe. Work together to make dinner, desserts, snacks, or cakes. Older kids can handle the main cooking tasks, while younger ones can help with measuring or decorating. It's a delicious way to spend time together!

7.   **Mini Worm Farm:** Create a worm farm using a large clear plastic container, soil, leaves, sand, and vegetable scraps. Layer the soil and sand (with soil layers being four times thicker than the sand) and top with vegetable bits and leaves. Add worms and place the container in a cool, dark spot for a few

days. The kids can observe the worms' tunneling and soil-churning activities. Remember to release the worms back into the wild when you're done.

8.   **Jewelry Making:** Collect beads, buttons, and string in a shoebox. When boredom strikes, bring out the box and let the kids make necklaces and bracelets. You can find plenty of beads and buttons from the rag-box to add to their creations.

9.   **Create a Picture:** Gather colorful magazines and small sheets of cardboard (A4 size works well). Give each child a piece of cardboard, some PVA glue, and magazines. Let them tear up the magazines and create mosaic pictures or collages.

10.   **Board Games:** Keep a variety of board games on hand, from simple to advanced. Spice up old favorites by playing under a blanket with a torch, under the table, in the shed, or with new "home-made" rules. Adding a twist

to familiar games makes them exciting again.

11. **Ghost Stories:** For a thrilling evening, gather torches/flashlights and cover a table with a heavy blanket. Crouch under the table with the lights and take turns telling ghost stories. The goal is to create the spookiest tales possible. Be prepared for a sleepless night, depending on the kids' ages!

12. **Growing a Seed:** Teach kids about plant growth in a fun way. Fold a paper towel into a medium-sized rectangle and dampen it. Place a seed between the first layer and the rest of the towel, then put the whole setup in a small plastic bag (like a Ziploc sandwich bag). Label the bags with the kids' names using masking tape. Place the bags in a slightly dark but accessible spot so the kids can watch their seeds sprout.

13. **Indoor Crazy Golf:** Design an in-door crazy golf course together, using toys, bathroom items, kitchen utensils,

or anything handy to create "holes" and routes. Small plastic golf sets are cheap and easy to find. Have treats ready for whenever a child completes the course.

2

OUTDOOR FUN

1. **Ribbon Sticks:** Create ribbon sticks using bamboo sticks and wide strips of ribbon. Cut 4ft sticks in half and tie a length of ribbon to one end, ensuring it's manageable for the kids. Let them use the sticks to create shapes, circles, and patterns like gymnasts on TV. This activity is a favorite of my 8-year-old with ADHD, keeping him engaged for extended periods.

2. **Garden Fun:** Invest in a cheap double-sided plastic sandbox for the garden. Fill one half with sand and the

other with water, and provide kitchen utensils and containers for endless playtime. Always cover the sandbox after use to prevent neighborhood cats from mistaking it for a litter box.

3.   **Berry Picking:** Find a berry-rich spot—blackberries, strawberries, red-currants, raspberries—and spend a day picking. Some places may charge, but many wild berries are free for picking. Make it educational by bringing along a book about berries to teach the kids which ones are safe and how to use them in desserts, jams, and cakes.

4.   **Treasure Hunt:** Organize a treasure hunt indoors, in the garden, at the park, or on a short walk. Hide small items, toys, or sweets, and create maps with "X Marks the Spot" and simple directions. Let the adventurous hunt begin!

5.   **Vegetable Patch:** Engage kids in gardening by creating a vegetable patch in your garden or a nearby space. Seeds

are affordable, and vegetables like carrots, lettuce, leeks, spring onions, and pumpkins are easy to grow. Herbs like watercress, parsley, chives, and basil are also simple and rewarding.

6.   **Nature Walks:** Take inexpensive nature walks with the kids, keeping them engaged by looking for specific plants, birds, or animals. Borrow books from the library about wildflowers, birds, or animals to enhance the learning experience. Equip each child with a notepad and pencil to jot down their discoveries.

7.   **Borrow A Pet:** Beat holiday boredom by involving kids with animals. If you don't have pets, offer to care for school gerbils, rabbits, or even your neighbor's dog during nature walks.

8.   **Camping Out:** Create lasting memories by camping in your backyard. Purchase affordable tents or craft a temporary one using sticks, sheets, and tarpaulin. Provide snacks, flashlights,

and sleeping bags for a night under the stars. Warn neighbors about potential noise and keep doors unlocked for comfort.

9. **Toy Sail Boats:** Craft toy sailboats from plastic bottles, wooden kebab sticks, and paper sails. Add weights like oil-based playdough to stabilize the boats. Take them to the nearest pond, stream, or bathtub for hours of sailing fun.

10. **Neighborhood Walk:** Explore your neighborhood with the kids to learn about local landmarks, parks, and historical buildings. Visit the library to research the area's history for an educational and entertaining outing.

11. **Ring Toss:** Make a ring toss game using plastic bottles filled with water, sand, or stones and painted paper plate rings. Set up a line for kids to stand behind and challenge them to toss rings over the bottles at varying distances.

Adjust the challenge as they step back
with each successful ring.

3

TRAVELING ACTIVITIES

1.   **Word Play:** Ideal for older kids learning to read, write, and spell. Take turns saying any word. The next person must start their word with the last letter of the previous word. For example, if someone says "engine," the next person could say "elephant," and so on. The challenge continues until someone can't think of a word starting with the required letter. The winner is the last person standing.

2.   **I Went To Market:** A memory game where players take turns saying, "I went

to market and I bought..." and add an item. The next person repeats the list and adds their own item. This continues until someone forgets an item. The last person to correctly recite the entire list wins.

3. **Find the Place:** Create a simple map of your route with city, town, and village names. Give each child a pen to check off each place as you pass it during the journey. It helps kids track progress and makes the journey more engaging.

4. **Car Colours:** Each child picks a car color and marks down every time they spot a car of that color. The first to reach a set number of sightings (e.g., 15 or 30 cars) wins. It's a great way to keep kids entertained and observant during trips.

5. **Alphabet Soup:** Players take turns naming words starting with consecutive letters of the alphabet (excluding X, U, and Z to simplify). Categories

like famous people, places, animals, or fruits can add a challenge. Keep going until someone can't think of a word for their letter.

6.   **Personal Bags:** Let each child pack a bag of their favorite toys and games for the journey. They can only take out one item at a time and play with it for a set time. Encourage swapping toys to keep things interesting, especially on longer trips.

7.   **Travel Diary:** Perfect for long journeys with stops. Each child gets a notepad and pen (or disposable camera for older kids, and art books for younger ones). They document the trip with drawings, notes about locations visited, and activities done. It keeps them occupied and provides a keepsake of the journey for reflection later on.